SHUHARI

A Spiritual Journey from Learning to Mastery

JOSHUA THADDEUS

Illustrated by
EVA POLAKOVIČOVÁ

SHUHARI: A Spiritual Journey from Learning to Mastery

© 2026 Joshua Thaddeus

joshuathaddeus.com | joshua@joshuathaddeus.com

Book cover art and design by Eva Polakovičová (evapola.com)

10 9 8 7 6 5 4 3 2 1

This book is for teachers, those who not only show the way, but help others to find their own.

For Mother—
my first and most enduring teacher.

CONTENTS

SHUHARI   I

STAGE ONE
WITNESS
守 SHU   7

STAGE TWO
APPROACH
破 HA   37

STAGE THREE
YIELD
離 RI   71

守 破 離   81

Acknowledgments   83
About the Author   85

SHUHARI

I'm going to paint you a portrait
you will not want to look upon.

Why not?

Because it is yours.

But I know myself.

You know a sketch of yourself.
I cannot tell you who you are,
but I can help you discover your true nature
as we paint your portrait together.

I can paint my own portrait.

Only through reflection,
your relationship with others,
are you introduced to yourself.
"YOU," the External.
"I," the Internal.
And the "SELF."
Only through "You" and "I"
can the Self be realized.

Do you know yourself?

You have shown me many things
I did not know.

What could I possibly teach you?

Everyone is a student,
everyone is a teacher,
and all are learning
in this eternal dance with one another.

Tell me about this dance.

It is the relationship you share
with the world around you.
The foundation of all relationships
is communication,
the art of expression.
If you are to dance,
you must be able to lead.
And in return...
follow.

I am not capable of such expression.

Of course you are.
You hide it out of fear.

Am I afraid to communicate?

You are afraid to be vulnerable.
You will, of course,
paint your own portrait.
But it will be enriched
by the color of those
with whom you surround yourself.

I am ready.
I am ready to paint my portrait.

You are not,
but none of us are.
The journey begins with desire.
Knowledge cannot be given;
it can only be accepted.

When the student is ready,
the teacher will appear.

When the student is truly ready...
the teacher will disappear.

— ANCIENT PROVERB

STAGE ONE
WITNESS

bear Witness...

Listen and learn, so that you may understand.

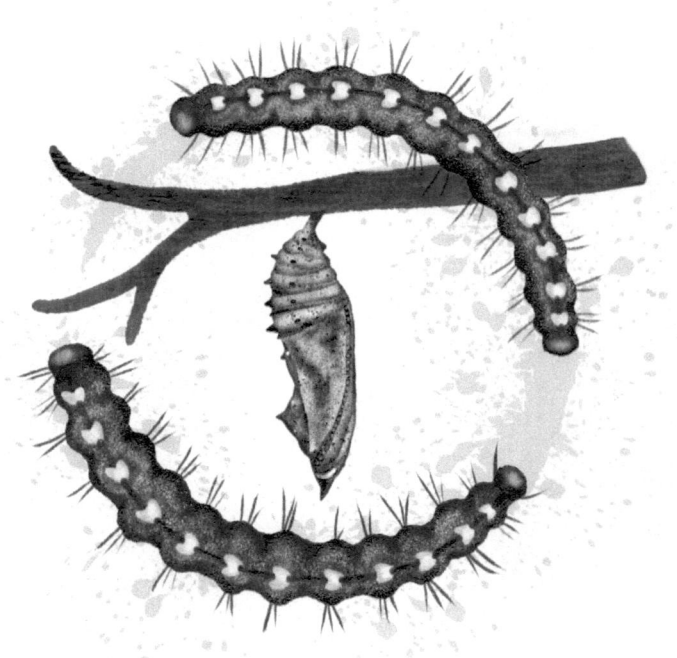

teacher leads—
student follows

Walk with me.
Let me show you the potential
you possess inside.

I walk alone—
I flounder.

Floundering...
a myriad of thoughts
emit an iridescent rainbow.
Something from the divide extends,
a tempting guide offering trust and betrayal.

From a black space,
a deep dark,
an eye gazes—
looking through a translucent surface
attached to the face of another.
Not a window,
but a reflection
glaring back into a soul.
It is "I."
A vision striking long and hard,
not distant—close,
as a presence that suddenly settles
like a limb recently realized.
Embracing the knowledge of another...
floundering.

You are caught in a prism,
wasting too much effort to escape
when there is no need.
Let me help,
let me show the way.

     I have what I need.
     What you have is of no use to me.

     Explore the path
     with curiosity and perception.

Acknowledge lessons as they unfold,
moving forward into the unknown.
Foolishly seek an answer
that is not known—
floundering.

Like a locked box,
the contents of which cannot be known...
until it is opened.
You have the key,
and yet are afraid of what is inside.

      I am not afraid.

In wanting,
a child reaches for fire
to touch the flames.
Another stretches from the inferno,
offering ideas—thoughts—lessons.
It burns...
to accept new ways—new paths—new truths.
It is "I"
being courted by "You"
in a dance.

To let go of what you have,
so that you may receive from others in kind,

is wise.

> I am fine with what I have,
> what I've gained in my time.
> These memories are mine.

Memory grows in the stories told
of experience shared with others.

> I do not need others to think for me.

You do not think for yourself
but of yourself.
You can get lost in thought.

> A reverie.

Until someone comes along and asks
what you're thinking about—

> Erasing my entire world.

> A teacher answers
> a student query.
> Not as an opponent,
> but a complimenting
> adversary.

Corresponding motion,
matching gestures,
a student follows
all directions—
until the teacher
poses questions.

Take my hand.
You can let go anytime you like.

> To what do I owe this engagement?
> I don't know that I can endure
> another messy arrangement.

After much debate
face-to-face,
we come to educate.
Some days will be bad
and some days will be good.
We challenge one another.
But our lessons
are mutually understood.

What worries you?

> It's not a matter of my moving on,
> but a dread that you will—

like others who, without cause,
left me reaching through the dark.

There doesn't have be a reason
they aren't with you,
a reason they left.
Reasons are often far and few.
People live their lives,
and sometimes two roads collide.
So you walk alongside—
until you stray.
Many of the people you meet
and the lessons they teach
are temporary.
Teachings are not all true.
Leave behind what is useless
and keep only what applies to you.

Self-expression:
Communication with self
and with others through mobility.
Another form of correspondence,
another form of expression.
To speak—
a conveyance of ideas
that come from a sense of—
Self-Expression.

Chosen without intent,
an unrestrained selection of
words, thoughts, and moves arise.
How is the choice made?
A considered response
or a charged reaction?
Expressing oneself freely—
is it a decision at all,
or something in the making,
that we become a conduit
forever educating?
Does the teacher influence
or is the student influenced?
Wisdom is but an offering
from a master to a pupil,
or a pupil unto a master.

What sacrifice must I make
to become a better,
more realized self?

Honesty,
admittance to ignorance.

There are many truths.

You must know

your own worst enemy.

> So, I must know myself
> if I am to become myself?

You must accept your truth.

> I've not yet become
> the person I want to know.

You are as you are.

> Do I not need improvement?

You cannot improve
on what you do not yet know.

> The foundation of faith
> sealed within an envelope
> is a heart.
> The obedience of a newborn child
> to crawl—to walk—to run
> is to lose the concept of self
> and trust that another
> will not let you fall.

> Could I not learn these lessons on my own?

It is a struggle
to put down words to express
what I am knowing,
if I know anything.
It is like a sickness
that will not go away,
a constant state of ignorance.

To find the cause of your own ignorance
is to be free of it.

What is it to learn, to obtain?
There is a fire inside me
I do not know.

Trapped in these worldly states,
we are backed into a corner of category.
To define someone
is to place them in a box
with no lock,
for we are impressionable.
This illusion of freedom
might not be illusion at all.
We don't have to keep ourselves
in these organized containers,
limiting the bounds of our behavior.
Change is possible

when it is believed.
But when a person is cast,
they tend to play a part
into which they were conceived.
Our own fear of change
keeps us from it.
Becoming another character
from the one we play
is a challenge—
To get away
from our own image.

You need not let go of your ideas.
But you must allow flexibility
to move beyond them.

        I don't know what I have,
        and, yet,
        I fear to lose it.
        Something deep inside
        calls to be nourished.
        Yet I cannot find it,
        unless it is shown to me.
        I watch, I ask, I listen,
        I touch, I gaze, I feel,
        I walk, I crawl, I run—
        I seek.

I fall into a trance,
deep into obscurity
as I suffer the instruction of another.
It will be my downfall
to be seduced,
both outward and within.
But I must become something of my own.
I must learn to die—
again.

To become yourself,
you must first let go of yourself.

I believe that I have.

There is no belief,
only faith—
in what you do not know.

You speak
as if I do not believe.
What could you possibly show me?

I have nothing to offer you.

But you are a master,
are you not?

A master
is only a reflection of the student.
And a master
knows only fear.

Fear of what?

Like a plateau
waiting to be passed,
each experience
means going beyond an inherent dread.

I can manage
what comes my way.

What matters
is how you deal with it.

How do I deal with it?

That is for you to tell me.
But with a proper foundation,
a platform
from which one has motivation,
one can at least
approach the lesson.

I seek a master to guide me.

It is not approval of a master you vie for,
but approval of self.

I do not understand.

There is nothing to understand,
simply respond
to what life demands.
When the moment comes,
and you have nothing to say—
that will be the moment
you find your way.
In the moment,
there is nothing to understand.

Connection becomes fluent
as the teacher takes the hand of the student.
The student follows instruction.
Slowly the teacher begins to back away
and return,
allowing the student to occasionally take lead.
The student bows
to the grace of the teacher.
They dance hand in hand.
They peruse one another's

sense of self.
The student does not challenge
the teacher's movements,
but resets to keep up.
Conforming without question
the student stresses
the teacher's motion.
In step—out step
as if looking into a mirror,
the teacher steps back
for the student to take the lead.
Uncertain of their next move,
the student stumbles.
Humbled,
the student gets up.
They continue to look at themselves
through the eyes of a teacher.
What went wrong?
Criticism—
from outer and inner voices,
will diminish or fuel the fire.

There is nothing out there
that will fix this mess.
Nothing out there
to take away my stress.

What is with you—in you—
is where your focus should rest.

> And I know the stars
> on my soul—they may never bless.
> Yet, I await them,
> nonetheless.

Feel it—
until it is done.
A hurting heart
is not a broken one.

> But I am broken.

Pain and experience make up your life.
But you must not let these experiences
dictate your life.
For to be possessed by your memories
is a path to corruption.
Pain is but fear
waiting to be exceeded,
advancing to the next plateau.
But there is no end.

> Life is a labyrinth.
> And I can't find my way.

Then let someone else show you.
The lesson is not about
finding the way out.
Allow yourself to be lost
and learn from that journey.
When you find another lost one
share in that misplacement
and choose a way together.

And when I come to a wall?

Change direction.

Floundering...

So easy to judge others.

When you see the world openly,
you see only yourself in others.

It never occurred to me
I could be a slave
to my own identity.
It never caught my attention
that the life I create
could become an obsession—
a portrait that holds my fate.

I know my name,
but I don't know my place.
Until I know where I stand,
I am betrayed by my face.

Are you your thoughts,
your dreams,
your memories?
If you were born to a different family,
would you still be you?
Are you really you,
or a caricature of yourself?
What makes you?
And what does, "YOU" mean?

Never was one to know myself.
I stare at my shadow like a stranger,
looking upon my reflection with suspicion.
I seek not to know myself,
but to forget all notion of identity,
until I am not but that
which moves through me.
But you see me, and in your eyes,
I am found—
afraid I am not but that which you made me.

Learn from others,

but do not allow others make you,
not even your teachers.
If you are to attain such transformation,
you must surrender to yourself
and only yourself.
You are never more you
than in that moment
when you are not yourself.

Who am I if I am not I?

Who you are
is not in question.
Who are you capable of being?
And you can be so much more.

I want to think I can—but I'm human.
And I think as such
that I'm not enough.

Your worth is not measured.
But your potential
is forever changing.

I don't like my portrait.

Then why should you expect anyone else to?

I'm exhausted—
tired of being hurt,
tired of hurting others.

Old habits are hard to break,
most of all
the cause of heartache.
If you want to change
who you are,
you have to let go of what you know.

But the deepest scars
are the most unforgettable.

You have to accept your truth.

What truth?

Remember when your soul was alive,
a time before someone sold you a lie?
You might accept the false reality.
But I can assure you of its fragility.
You listened because you are mortal,
bound to doubt yourself.

I want to think I can—but I'm human.

And so am I, like anyone else.
But we live in the tales we tell ourselves.

How do I find my tale, my truth?

You must step aside,
out of your own way.

To know when I am ready
is to be ready.
My thoughts—I don't know
how they come and where they go.
The death of ideas
leaves me with nothing to show.
As thoughts return,
memory leaves me
dancing in the dark
with the same ideas
again and again—
until I remember my sins.

And then you will be ready
to exceed limitations.
Only when you have learned,
when you have accepted those limitations,
will you be able to move past them.

Before noon, after dawn
and again at five.
At half-past, we spoke.
You listened to another,
and it was not I.

Ten minutes pass…
you brush, I follow.

Then we paint, hand in hand
'til I follow another.
You plainly speak,
and I may very well hear.

Quarter to six…
I stroke. You don't follow.

My hand hurts, I need rest, I stop.
You kept painting
and so did I.
I consider the composition of the canvas.
Then, what do you care?
Why do I feel so obliged
to portray the one you recognize?
What do I care, but for myself?

I do not speak.

Yet, you listen.

Five past six...

Damn it, I'm late!
Seduced by your wisdom,
I am cursed by your charm.
But it is your knowledge
I desire.

We paint at dusk and just before seven
five to seven...

You stare,
with approval in your eye.
Silent am I.
I choose to pick up a brush.
I paint the subject.
You gaze at me.
In your eye—
I become lost.
And as you draw—
so do I.

Seven o' clock

Where do we go from here?

> It's a tragic dance,
> the game of chance.
> Of who you encounter
> and where you stand.

Assigned a role—
of which I am to portray.
A mission—
from which to begin,
equipped with what tools I am given—
without much say.

> You decide how to play.

The role I've been assigned
does not align with my design.

> Your age is a stage,
> a track of your time.
> As you grow
> adjust your understanding,
> in line with your state of mind.
> Hesitate—

but don't dwell on mistakes.
How you choose
to respond to your fate
is for you to debate.
So, what's life going to be?
Something you accept—
or something you decree?

For I am not you.

And you are not I.

Neither are we anything but what we are.

The brightest among the stars,
I never feel so radiant
than when I am eclipsed by Luna.
Through space I drift,
glowing among gloom;
awaiting your shadow,
until I am again consumed.
I share with you my light of my day
and all you do
is reflect it away.
This portrait is not mine.

It is you.

You have buried your self-image
so deep, to the point
you don't remember who you are.

Inspiration will come to me,
eventually.

Patience is not the same as idleness.
Time is not your friend.
Time will leave you,
again and again.
Time will never listen
when you ask for more.
Your pleas—
time will always ignore.
Time will make dreams come true
but not to last.
Of dreams—
time will make memories past.
You must not be idle.

I'm trapped
in ways I cannot explain.
So used to pain,
I'm not sure it will change—

Change is the only constant,

like dying.

I do not know death.

> If you want to truly live,
> you must first learn to die.

What am I dying for?

> A student does not seek answers,
> for their lessons are that alone.

I learn only so that I can,
but to what end?
Trying to understand where I stand,
I feel small
in the scope of it all.
The picture is not so plain to see
as I trace and I paint
my identity.
I cannot convey
the moods as they relay.
Like predicting the rain,
I go from calm to storm
at a moment's display.
What will my mood be tomorrow?
Well—

it's hard to say.
The world revolves,
and I feel its rotation.
Gravity draws me to meet elation
until I hit rock bottom,
before I blossom.
Do you not see the gall
of my situation?

   Trust that another will guide.

Ambiguous thoughts get in my head,
so I trust my feelings instead.
But my portrait does not comply
with the person I am on the inside.

   As long as you seek,
   you shall never find.

STAGE TWO
APPROACH

choose your Approach...

Question what you understand,
so that you may know.

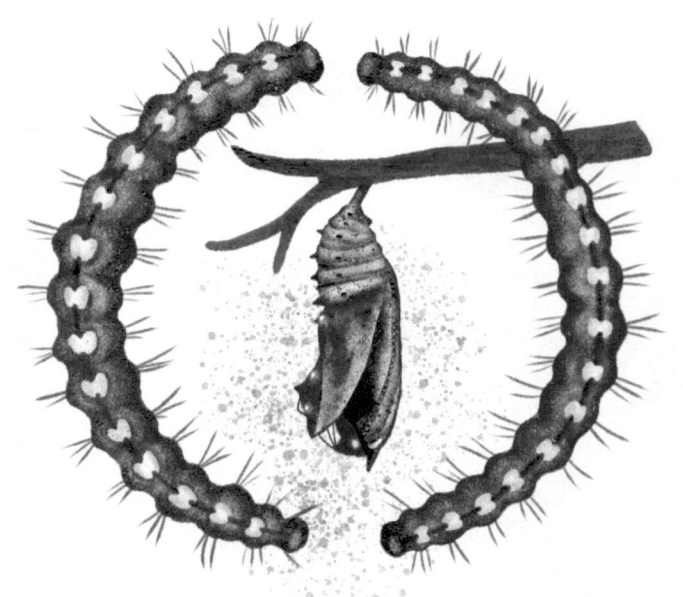

破HA

A beating in my heart,
of which I'm in denial.
The rhythm I still hear
it patters once in a while.
To which I have grown
callused and numb,
and nothing I've done
is worthwhile.
My portrait is but an echo
of a smile.

Alone—
content with despair.
Though, deep in your heart,
a longing to share.
Behind a wall,
you crawl,
as your heartbeat stumbles;
at another's touch
the barrier crumbles.
Shards fall—
shattering your soul.
You gather the pieces
to hang your portrait whole,
hidden—
behind a wall.

I hide nothing.

You hide from those with whom
you will not share your teachings.

So much arrogance.
Would a master have such ego?

This world needs input,
including your own.

And what of those
that succumb to solitude?

>You have something to show yourself—
>as much as those around you.

I have all I need within.

>But you know nothing of yourself.
>Sometimes
>you need someone else to show you
>how to unlock
>what is inside of you.

I can see it right here,
in my own portrait.

>You lie to yourself.

I am indecisive?

>You are in conflict.
>You are not defined by conflict,
>but you are recognized
>by how you respond to it.

I know

what I want to convey.

So respond.

I'm sorry
I'm just not ready.

You are prepared,
yet you are still afraid.

I fear that it will come out wrong.

Stop acting like you're special,
like you are the only one
that makes mistakes.
It's what we do.
It's what we must do
so that we can improve.

I want to think I can—

Don't be so hard on yourself.
Your misery is arrogance.
You think you're special.
You think you're supposed to be great.
You can't stand the idea
of being average.

but I'm human.

> You will let pain rule your life.
> But at some point,
> whether it takes a day or a decade,
> you have to get over it
> and stop using it
> as an excuse for stagnancy.

And I think as such
that I'm not enough.

> You want to be special?
> Do something that few do:
> accept your mistakes.
> That doesn't mean blame yourself
> or feel sorry for yourself.
> It means acknowledge your problems—
> and move on.
> That would be special.
> But you are not special,
> and you are not asked to be.

I want to be you.

> You lift me up
> like some kind of hero.

I've heard the stories
of how you earned your halo.

> You think me divine,
> a model for how to survive—
> before you lie?
> You look at me,
> as you look to the stars
> above the sky.

I'm just a mortal,
with wings that cannot fly.

> Were it that my wings
> did not fly,
> that my halo
> did not glow,
> that angels were only
> made of snow?
> That I be loved
> on my level,
> neither as angel...
> or devil.
> Would that others
> did not judge me
> for the span of my wings—
> or the radiance of my ring.

I just want to be more
than a human being.

>   In every travesty
>   there is a hidden beauty,
>   catharsis forged in hell—

Where I often dwell.

>   Demons were born angels
>   until they fell.

And I—
know this all too well.

>   Beauty is sometimes ugly
>   and often has claws.
>   In your pursuit of perfection
>   you miss the charm in your flaws,
>   the little quirks you don't regard.
>   You see divinity,
>   but just like you—

I'm ordinary.

>   That's not a bad thing.
>   You have to earn the scars

that will carry you
  further than your wings.

Defiance is the province of an angel
deterring from the known road
to find solace.
The most convincing illusion
is drawn from reality;
a lie embellished upon truth to make life,
the deep nothing,
more appealing.
Making one's own way—
a meandering of self
in order to find the self.
The "I" at war with the "You."
Meandering...
lost without guide,
through endless winds.

I want to change.
But I do not know how.
I do not know how to let go
because I am holding on—
to a way, a way that I cannot find.
I have surrendered to solitude.
If I could only let go of my mind.

Meandering...
through a myriad of destinations.
Looking for one when there is none.
Picking a grain of sand
as if separated from the rest.
There is no distinction
because they are the same.
The teacher and student
walk hand in hand
until one of them breaks away.
An angel
leaves an angel
to dance with a devil.

"I" am alone without "You."
But alone
is the only way I can learn
who I am.

> You can sketch me,
> but you cannot paint me.
> To draw "you,"
> you must first forget
> "yourself."

I cannot do this.

There is an art to dying.

As if I were ever really here?

You were never here before.

But I am here now.

Let go of preconceived notions of self,
as though you never existed.
Unlearn all that has been learned.

How does one step
out of one's own way
to find the cause of one's own ignorance?

With the help of another.
A teacher must lose awareness,
to make the student aware.

As one studies, so does one teach.
As one listens, so does one speak.
As one takes, so does one also give.

For I am not I.

And You are not You.

Neither are we anything but what we are.

How angry can I be at my adversary?
How upset can I be with myself
if I am shaped in response
to the opposition of my enemies,
internal and external?
If I am to see myself
in response to my challenger,
how angry can I be at my transgressor?
If I am to admit that those who challenge me
in turn shape me,
perhaps evil is inevitable.
Are failure and tragedy
necessary colors of a portrait?
It is a selfish viewpoint
that I am the protagonist of my story.
Do I thank my opponent?
Is my adversary also my teacher?
Am I myself, not also—
an enemy of my enemy?
Is it destiny
to always suffer an opposing force?
If it is true,
how angry can I be at my adversary,
how angry can I be at myself,
if I am shaped by my response to them?

Still,
would I rather no conflict at all?
Who would I be,
without something to oppose me,
to keep me in check?
How can I grow alone
without reflection to show me who I am?
It's not only external,
but internal unrest as well.
Perhaps external evil
is acted out by those
who have felt so defeated through internal conflict.
They seek victory—
over something outside themselves?
These internal, external voices
have only strengthened my resolve
and complemented my own portrait.
How can I know my limits
until they are pushed?
I need to know that I fight conflict
and make a conscious decision every day.
I need to know that my decisions are chosen
and not just my innate behavior.
Am I who I am?
Or can I decide who I want to be?
From my enemy's perspective,
does intent matter?

If one truly believes in one's purpose
—good or evil—
does it matter who or why another opposes?
Whatever I stand for, conflict will arise.
And I will face it.
Such moments define who I am,
painting the strokes of my portrait.

> You must remember to forget
> in order to release your conflicts.
> Learn from them,
> then let them go,
> or they will consume you.

Have I abandoned myself to contentment?
Have I given up on myself,
chasing what I already know?
Perhaps my inner teacher is dormant,
resting like a sleeping monster
to one day be awakened
with fervor and ferocity?
Deep inside me are a fire
and a storm
determined to consume one another.
I struggle great internal conflict
and it paves the path set before me.

Your journey is ahead
but your destination is behind.

I cannot see
what is behind me.

When you cannot find your way,
you simply—turn around.

I become a master
simply by changing direction?

Teaching
is the only route to mastery.
In teaching,
you see yourself through a mirror
reflected by your student.
You, in turn—
better understand yourself
in being taught by the student.

To become a master,
I need to again become a student?

You become a master
when you follow a student.

Will you follow me?

       It is time to take my leave.

Are you disappointed?

       Of course not.

Then why would you leave me?

       It has nothing to do with you.
       You're ready to walk on your own—
       or, rather, follow others.

I am afraid to walk alone.

       You never stop being afraid.
       No, I cannot follow you.
       But the lessons we have shared
       will always be with you,
       as long as you wish to carry them.

I miss the point.

       There is no point.
       There is only plateau.
       You must move past it.

The challenge of letting go
is no challenge at all,
for no work is implied.
Letting go
is a state of having let go.
It is no challenge,
because there is nothing to challenge.
There is nothing to let go.
We are in constant defiance.
But we must release
that defiance.
Not to forget,
but to move through it.
We cannot stay angry.
We cannot stay
in that state of defiance.

Where will I go?

> Wherever you will,
> but without me.

I don't care where I go,
so long as it is with you.

> You will not walk alone.
> But you must move on—

for yourself.
In others, recognize yourself.
But remember:
that you are not everyone else.

I need you to finish my portrait.

Your portrait is enriched
by the color of those
with whom you surround yourself.
But your portrait is still yours—
you finish it.

I want to think I can—but I'm human.
And I think as such
that I'm not enough.
I feel sucker-punched,
and it's rough.
Every lesson gets harder
before it gets better.
But if there is a way,
can we not find it together?
So don't leave me.
Teach me,
not for the benefit of knowledge,
but for the sake of my soul.
Only with you can I discover

who I am down this road.
Perhaps in time
another will come along
whose path crosses with my own.
But you don't have to leave me alone.
Why must you run from me,
leave me confronting
the things I don't know?
I appreciate your guidance.
You have my compliance.
But I can't stop this feeling
of a transparent ceiling,
that there's only so far
I can go.
I want to think I can—but I'm human.

Accept that love
is transient.
Life is a series of affairs
that end unexpectedly.
We all go at our own pace,
and the best you can do
is look next to yourself.
See who is there with you—
rather than ahead or behind.
People come and go
in our lives.

When you're young
you think of love as forever.
Then you get older,
and you enjoy it as it comes.
And then you realize—
love is now,
love is present.
And if you are ever loved by someone
their lessons
remain with you.

Who am I without you?

Our lesson is over.
It's time to grow up—
and exhibit the portrait you tore apart.

I can't wipe the ink stain from my hands.

That's not ink,
but blood on your hands,
revealing the pain
you won't pour on the canvas.
Perhaps you're not yet ready to show,
hiding behind
what you think you know.

There is nothing tell.

> In spite of what you believe,
> it is yourself you deceive—
> when you deprive others of your stories.

I have little to offer,
and much to lose.

> It's easy to keep—and to take—
> but now you must give something away.

The lessons are mine to apply.

> Those classes you took,
> what you read in a book—
> just glasses
> through which to look.
> Stop twisting stories you didn't write
> to shape your life.
> And share—
> in the tales of others
> and their sacrifice.
> It's hard work, farming the soil,
> after much has been spoiled.
> So, take a time, a sabbath
> to reflect on your sorrow,

and get ready to master tomorrow.

I'm no teacher.

Then I am no student.

For you are not I.

And I am not you.

Neither are we anything but what we are.

Am I to teach you?

Do you want to?

Why should I suffer the burden of sight
that would show the way,
rather than dwell in blind delight?

Let me show you the way.

I do not see.

Do not be discouraged in the dark,
lest light is traveling behind.
The black is not to fear
before a shadow has arrived.
That which is unseen
is not that which is unknown.
For there is worse than darkness
among sins to atone.
Light you will find
when you open your mind
to that—
which you cannot see.
But the ways that are shown

may not be—
exactly what they seem.

How does one come to this place?

I have been a student for so long,
I'm not even sure if I know anything.
I thought I was important—
as we all do
until we are faced with reality.
And trust me, teacher, you will be.

I am not afraid of reality.

You should be.

I have conquered fear.

Conquering is dull.
To conquer—
is true death.
For it kills the curiosity
that keeps you alive.
When you no longer want,
then you truly die.
Surely you want something.

I want to let go.

But you fear to?

How can I not?

It's okay to be afraid.
It's not about being unafraid
but accepting change as part of life.
Only then
can you face your true opponent.

I thought to face you.

You face yourself.
You face
your own shadow,
your own doubt.

And others before me?

We become stuck
when we are unable
to bear the burden of loss.
So often
we succumb to solitude,
not realizing

we have made ourselves
prisoners.
We are free
when we allow ourselves
to be vulnerable.

How have you managed
to free yourself?

I have submitted to solitude.

You've embraced
your own ignorance.
Yet you just spoke
otherwise.

I can teach values
I do not aspire to.

You will, of course,
paint your own portrait.
But it will be enriched
by the color of those
with whom you surround yourself.

I have no control of others.

I do not think you lack control
so much as patience.

       I feel the void of loneliness
       all the time,
       even in the company of others.

Loneliness is a lie.
None of us are alone,
especially not in the company of ourselves.
We just need to be reminded of that.

       I have only learned pain
       from others.

Heartbreak can be a beautiful thing.
This pain, this emptiness,
is also a pain you feel
when you care for others.

       I have nothing to gain
       from others.

You're always learning,
even when you're alone.
But sometimes you need to stop,
shut up,

and listen to others—
or to yourself.

> I've walked away
> from all others.

Whenever you walk away
from someone in this life
remember what you gained from them.

> You don't get rest by holding on.
> You get rest
> by letting go.

Relationships are...
self-study
as much as anything.
Ultimately, we're getting to know ourselves
through our relationships
with others.

> I prefer my own company.

Tell me something
you have gained from solitude.

> There are the chance encounters

with strangers.

So, you are open to others?

>I am shackled
>by my own chains
>until another sets me free.

Only you can free yourself.

>I thought
>I could not do it alone.

I can show you how,
but I can't do it for you.

>Where must I go now?

Where teachers cannot follow.

>I can see your grief.
>You have suffered great loss.

Loss—
that I want to teach
and learn from in return.

What awaits me
once I release my chains?

Whatever awaits you
is up to you.
But you will not master it
if you are not prepared to let go.

I have only sacrificed.
I don't even know for what.
What honor is in death?

It is the most honorable thing we do.
Our world is built in cycles.
Everything that is born
is birthed
knowing it will not last.
What is honorable
is acknowledging that your time
is limited,
giving a stronger appreciation for what you have
while you have it.
How does one celebrate life
and not in turn celebrate death?
We all come to defeat eventually.
I'm not talking about loss,
but time.

And ours is simply up.

Why bother living at all?

To learn.

And you are a hypocrite.
You can move on as well.
You're just afraid,
suffering solitude
like the rest of us.

I am afraid.
Alone,
I am whoever I paint myself to be.
In company—
there are no colors I see,
but for the canvas
on which they portray me.

I thought
you had all the answers.

An intelligent mind
is an inquiring mind.
It is not satisfied with explanations
or conclusions.

Nor is it a mind that believes,
because belief is, again,
another form of assumption.

>And to face death
>in that uncertainty?

Is to have faith

>—in something greater than the self.

Like you,

>I am nothing.

>When we realize this, we transcend everything.

STAGE THREE
YIELD

Yield to your true nature...

Let go of what you know, so that you may transcend.

teacher and student become one

Art is a conversation,
an open discourse
evoking thoughts—a lesson.
Our lives are an ongoing expression.
It doesn't matter how something is conveyed.
What matters is how it is received.

Images come into focus
rather than being sought out.
We have a correspondence with objects
as we do with others.
The world is a series of relationships.
How we relate to things

or respond to them
defines us.

Creation is not to fill space
but complement it.
We see blank space and insist on filling it.
The space is there to offer,
not to fill.

We're all a little empty inside,
and so we fill space.
Our condition
is feeling so compelled
to convey the human condition—
to fill space.

A building
with barren halls:
so you sweep floors,
clean the windows,
and paint the walls
until it doesn't feel so small.

You keep busy, so you don't have to look
at what you cannot bear.
In the corner of your stare,
that empty chair:

the one you left open
for the one who sat there.

You go back to a memory
—revisit—
like returning home after time away:
it's familiar,
and also entirely new.

It's an encounter:
finding your way back
to a person that loved you;
once familiar,
now a ghost that haunts you.

You have a thought
and it skips—
like a glitch,
a gap in your mind
you can never refill.
And you're desperate to get back there,
to get lost—
And so we talk to fill the space.

But words can never do justice.
They cannot speak
for the thoughts, wants, needs, ideas,

feelings, and experiences of us.
Absolutely nothing can words truly entail.
But at least they might intrigue the mind
to expand and explore the hearts desire.

Quickly words come, and faster they go;
from one moment to before you know.
Words are but comfort, sometimes pain.
They are powerful and deceiving,
harmful and relieving.
We are often lost of words,
yet they are unceasing.
We communicate with them,
yet they do not communicate but through us.
And never can words do justice.

It's all nonsense—
saying a lot
without having anything to say at all.

So we fill space.
Art is how we relate to the world.
We spend so much time
painting a portrait,
filling space.

So rarely do we simply express

one brushstroke at a time
without trying to convey some deeper
meaning.
So rarely do we just live
without the thought of dying.

The only art is dying.
For it is the craft
a lifetime is spent mastering.

This idea—
that we're wasting time—
should never cross our minds.
We get older and we need reasons
as to how or why we do things.
Because we're afraid
that what we're doing doesn't matter.
But it all matters.
Your life—
matters.

Infancy is the way to infinity.
The beginning never ends.
We never stop learning
but we often stop practicing
because we cannot stand to lose.

Defeat is the great teacher,
but we don't have to master it.
Mastering comes at the moment
we realize there is nothing to master
because we have no control,
only our response.

We are not defined by conflict
but we are shaped
by our response to it—
to others
to the world around us
to ourselves.

As a conduit of art
there is nothing I need do
but receive
and transmit to you.

Accept defeat, learn to lose
You can try to avoid it,
but pain is a part of you
It's okay to crawl into that chrysalis
to hide for a time.
But only through conflict
can you become the butterfly.

And that suffering is a bridge to others,
a pain shared with our sisters and brothers.
Hand to your chest,
touch the rhythm breathing.
And you feel it then—listen
to the heart beating.
Your eyes swell
from the love you are feeling.
You thank God for
the days repeating—
drifting off to join them,
the people dreaming.

In constant correlation,
we are at the mercy of others.
For so long as another questions,
you must answer
the sound of a voice calling your name.

Enjoy a conversation with yourself
or with a friend.
Answer a call from your parent,
or call out to your child.
Look into the eyes of someone
who makes you smile.
Reply to the unexpected letter.
Encourage others to feel better.

Accept a gift from someone
you didn't know cared.
Engage in silly gossip your sibling shares.
Under a shelter, in bad weather,
have awkward banter with a stranger
to bear the pain you're feeling together.
Hold a hand
when you are afraid.
Help someone clean up
the mess they've made.
Listen to the subtle sound, an innuendo.
Life is in the small talk,
the soft echoes
in between romantic crescendos.

If you want to master death,
you only have to live.

Wait for the clouds to clear,
for the sun to shine,
and rainbows to appear.
Only rain remains,
a broken promise all the same.

Only the rain remains,
and we're left with this pain.
Then another comes with an umbrella

and brings it overhead.

Still, only the rain remains,
but now it doesn't seem so sad.

We see the world from different places
and correspond with many faces
as we navigate difficult spaces.
Though our feelings are not always mutual,
these variances are beneficial.
For we're all part of the same circle.
People of all shapes, styles, and colors,
teaching and learning from each other.

The self paints no portrait but that of another.

Tracing the brush path,
bristles wear away in ink—
a butterfly strokes.

守 破 離

守 SHU

破 HA

離 RI

ACKNOWLEDGMENTS

This book would not exist without the constant lessons I've learned from my family. Thank you for teaching me every day, for believing in me, and for giving me the freedom to grow.

Thanks to God, whose presence gives me the strength to create when the path feels unclear.

Thank you, Eva, whose incredible illustrations elevated this work beyond what I imagined. To my editors, Michael and Austin, who offered invaluable insight throughout this process.

And finally, to the readers: thank you to everyone who opens Shuhari. May these words guide you on your journey, as the people mentioned here have guided me.

ABOUT THE AUTHOR

Learn more about Joshua Thaddeus. Subscribe to the author's newsletter for updates on upcoming books (Foster Poems & Color Sketches) at his website:

JoshuaThaddeus.com

Joshua Thaddeus is a New Orleans–based author and philosophical soul whose work invites readers to explore their inner worlds through thought-provoking narration. For as long as he can remember, writing has been a cathartic outlet for his spiritual curiosity. When not contemplating the universe through poetry, this introspective writer dabbles in Japanese calligraphy (書道, Shodō) and ink painting (墨絵, Sumi-e). Through storytelling, Joshua reflects on human nature, exploring the mysteries within us.